PROGRESS NOTES
MADE SIMPLE

Lakeeya Homsey, LICSW

TABLE OF CONTENTS

ABOUT THE AUTHOR

L akeeya Natasha is a Licensed Independent Clinical Social Worker (LICSW), therapist, author, motivational speaker and life coach. Lakeeya holds an Associate's degree in Behavioral Health and Human Sciences (BHHS) from the Community College of Philadelphia and both Bachelor's and Master's degrees in Social Work from Temple University.

Determined to not let her beginning dictate her ending, Lakeeya used her experiences as a little girl from the inner city, to create a platform to inspire other at-risk populations to work hard and dream big. She began the process of regaining her power by telling the truth about her childhood abusers. Having adults in her life making unhealthy choices and not being supported when she came forward, left her vulnerable to other predators and lead to years of untreated mental health issues including several suicide attempts. Lakeeya recognized no one would give her the freedom she longed for so she fought for it and claimed it as hers. Having good and consistent talk therapy and redefining her relationship with God is how she fought back. She fights back those thoughts of inadequacy and victimhood daily. She shares that hope with all she comes in contact with whether in a group home, homeless shelters, office settings or the Philadelphia Prison System. All of her clients learn that freedom is not a place; it is a mindset.

After recovering from a toxic and abusive first marriage and unhappy with the dating scene she got marriage for the second time. Recognizing she craved the stability that marriage could bring to her children and her desire to be a "good wife", Lakeeya became the CEO and co-founder of the Love Train Experience. The organization demonstrates the reality of marriage and promotes happy, healthy relationships. From 2013 to 2019, the Love Train has hosted eight committed couple retreats, six adult game nights and countless date night outs events. The goal of the organization was simple "to have more people choose healthy partnerships and to make commitment fun." Unfortunately, and fortunately, working with other couples, she realized that though her second marriage was not abusive, it was definitely toxic, because she was left lonely and vulnerable by a man that said he was her husband. She began 2020, as a newly separated woman yet again and decided it was best to discontinue her work with the Love Train because the work, she did with other couples, was not a reflection her own relationship.

Lakeeya knows from both personal and professional experiences that 1) acknowledging one has a problem is the hardest step to healing and 2) finding healthy support and accountability partner is the second. She launched her own private practice with this in mind.

Transitions4Life, LLC offers mobile and e-therapy (text, call, email, and video) to minimize excuses from busy working professionals. Through Transitions4Life, Lakeeya assist individuals, families, couples, and other helping professionals in becoming more aware of specific patterns that are keeping them stuck and preventing them from moving forward. She provides the tools and strategies that women and men need to overcome their obstacles to live their best lives and define their version of freedom.

Along with private clinical practice, Lakeeya used the tips in her small book series to become one of the youngest and highest paid clinical supervisors of a large non-profit community mental health agency. Covid-19 shifted how everyone did business and because Transitions4Life was already set up as a telehealth practice, it took off and surpassed its financial benchmarks. Having great organization and drive, Lakeeya was able to maintain and grow her practice of one while working full time for the other organization. That all changed suddenly.

In March 2021, as she was on medical leave, she received a call from the HR department saying she was terminated. She found out a few weeks later, that the company went into bankruptcy and closed. Having her own business already, she was taken back emotionally but not knock down financially. That experience solidified the notion that jobs are not loyal to no one but itself and we as a people need to be loyal to ourselves, our purpose, and people attached to us over any job. Additionally, it became even more important for Lakeeya Natasha to help others succeed in business even if it is just a secondary income because this Post Pandemic life brings so much uncertainty.

Lakeeya credits her faith in God for her ability to push past her pain to find her purpose. She understands that her life and her story are not her own. They are meant to be shared to set others held captive free.

This story has a happy ending, for she finally found her person! She married her best friend and new business partner, Walter Homsey, on May 24, 2022. Both are licensed therapists wanting to help people find personal freedom through connection with their higher selves, nature, and re-establishing sense of community. They created a platform to do just that called One Trip Over the Moon. Through One Trip Over the Moon, the couple offers a holistic approach to healing and embracing a life full of peace and joy.

For more information about **Transitions4Life, LLC**, please contact: askkeeya@gmail.com or follow us on Facebook & Instagram.

For more information about **One Trip Over the Moon, LLC**, contact onetripoverthemoon@gmail.com or follow us on Facebook, Instagram, & Twitter.

DISCLAIMER:

The templates, in this book, are to be used as tools to assist Clinicians in writing therapeutic notes in a timely manner. **The tools should never be used instead of clinical judgment.** All notes should be tailored for individual Client circumstances and needs using your best clinical judgment for that individual. As part of that, you should personalize notes by making sure you note the Client's name with the pertinent information gathered in each session. For that reason, I do not suggest anyone just copy and pasting the notes from this book but use as a guideline.

NOTE: *This book and other clinical books written by author uses the term "client" yet it is understood that many organizations and agencies use terms like consumers, patients, or participants. Follow the language of where you are employed. If you are a private practice- use your discretion.*

NOTE: *Adding the client's name, their preferred pronouns, and their personal quotes from each session will help to personalize your notes and is recommended.*

NOTE: *Do not assume, no matter what the client looks like, please ask what is their preferred pronoun during the introduction and used that pronoun in documentation. This honors the person and helps them feel seen and validated. In this book, she/he is used. I am aware and recognize that there are other pronouns. This was only for the sake of clarity and conciseness.*

INTRODUCTION

To become (and be known) as a competent Clinician, one must learn all of the components of good clinical practice. You may be great in some areas and need more supervision in others. It is completely normal. The one universal mountain to climb for all Clinicians is documentation. The one who can conquer their paperwork can conquer their day.

Just saying the word-"**paperwork**" and writing down makes me cringe. I don't know if any counselor who likes it: intakes, assessment summaries, recovery plans, treatment plans, safety plans, progress notes, group notes, discharge summaries and court reports.

We did not get into this field to do paperwork, but some days, it is all we do. Paperwork can consume our lives. Many counselors complete paperwork on their days off, during family time and even during vacation. We all know that paperwork is the way we secure our payments and often times keeps us employed. However, it doesn't make it any easier to complete.

Documentation does not have to get the best of you. Quitting a job because of the paperwork only to find that the next job has its fair share of documentation is disheartening. No one should be obligated to complete paperwork outside of work day hours, but in the beginning of my clinical career I spent many of nights catching up on notes. I decided this process was actually hindering my clinical growth and my personal life.

There are ways to set yourself up so that documentation won't beat you.

First, gain an understanding of every document in your organization. If there are any redundant forms or processes, discuss them with your supervisor. There may be a way to integrate documents that hadn't been considered before. However, if you are told there is a good reason for similar forms to be completed for one client, ask your supervisor for further explanation to gain a better understanding. (Most likely, it can be related to billing for services.)

Second, use good time management and organization skills. I found that many of my colleagues that struggle with paperwork are the ones who wait until the end of the day (or worse the end of the week) to complete their notes. Save a few minutes at the end of the session to review with the client what was discussed and plan for the next appointment. Write everything down immediately. Once the client leaves the office, spend a few minutes finishing the notes.

Lastly, understand what is required for good notes. Learn the structure and then create templates for general topics and assessments. This will cut down on your time rewriting similar notes. **Appendix B** is a handout I created **(Good Notes Have Good Structure)** for those I supervised to that they can understand the structure of good notes.

The templates included in this book helped me decrease the feeling of being burned out and gave me more time to focus on improving my clinical practice and become a *Goal Chaser!*

To learn more about becoming a Goal Chaser: improving our clinical practice and accomplishing your professional goals, read another book in this book series entitled *"The Goal Chaser's Guide to Clinical Practice".* (The third book is *"Treatment Planning Made Simple".)*

RISK ASSESSMENT – HOW TO INDICATE AND DOCUMENT RISK LEVELS

E very agency organization has their own lingo. Risk Assessment is sometimes called Suicide Risk Assessment, Assessment for Safety, Assessment Summary or any number of other names. It can be an individual form or included as part of a Biopsychosocial, Recovery Plan or Discharge Summary.

No matter what the name, this assessment is very important. It determines the stability of a client during an evaluation or scheduled session. It can determine the level of care recommended or whether a person is in need of crisis intervention.

This assessment is always reviewed if something goes wrong with a client's treatment or if a person is involuntarily committed. Therefore, it can be a nerve wrecking experience for clinicians to word a person's disposition in a way that could be scrutinized by clinical teams and hold up in a court of law.

Before we dive into the Progress Notes, let's review some tips and examples to help simplify your Assessments.

Assessments Made Simple

Ask yourself Who, What, When, Where, Why and How:

o **Who** can give you information about your client' disposition prior to coming to the session?

o **What** prompted the need for the assessment?

o **When** did the symptoms begin? **When**, if any, was the last time the client felt safe or unstable?

o **Where** is your client's focus? (Are they aware (oriented) of their surroundings or are they distracted by internal stimuli?)

o **Why** is your client in need of additional safety measures? Or, **Why** not?

o **How** will they have services delivered to them (Voluntarily, Involuntarily, Inpatient, Outpatient, Partial, IOP, Residential, ACT)

If you can answer these questions, you can complete a Risk Assessment.

If you work in community mental health or within a multi-disciplinary team, you should write enough information to give future providers/clinicians an idea of what the client's baseline level of functioning is and identify indicators of imminent crisis or an episode of instability.

Make sure the level of risk is clear: LOW, MODERATE (AT-RISK), OR HIGH. Here are some examples of assessment notes:

o **LOW RISK -** "Currently LOW RISK as evidenced by no current suicidal or homicidal ideations, no auditory or visual hallucinations, no visible instability or risk for withdrawal. Mood and affect appropriate. Oriented 3x. Thoughts were logical and linear throughout interview and maintained good eye contact. Recommended to continue outpatient mental health services due to history and current stressors as well as referral to psychiatric prescriber for evaluation for the appropriateness of medication and medication management."

o **MODERATE RISK** – "Currently MODERATE RISK evidenced by passive suicidal or homicidal ideations with no intent or plan, auditory or visual hallucinations present but not yet affecting ability to function, no visible instability or risk for withdrawal imminent. Mood and affect are appropriate. Oriented 3x. Thoughts were logical and linear throughout interview and maintained good eye contact. Recommended to continue outpatient mental health services and assessment for higher level of care needs. Due to history and current stressors, increase sessions to weekly as well as referral to psychiatric prescriber for evaluation for the appropriateness of medication and medication management."

- o **HIGH RISK -** "Currently HIGH RISK evidenced by active suicidal or homicidal ideations with intent and plan, auditory or visual hallucinations, visible instability (or risk of withdrawal imminent). Mood and affect (questionable/flat/blunt/depressed/manic). Oriented 3x. Poor insight and poor judgment present. Recommended to be evaluated for higher level of care. Risk of self-harm or harm of others imminent without additional intervention. Hospitalization/Detox was discussed. Client was: agreeable, defensive, combative or refused care. The following action was taken…"

Hopefully, the above information will be helpful in completing your risk assessments. Now let's discuss simplifying the progress notes generated from these assessments.

PROGRESS NOTES
MADE SIMPLE

As a Clinical Supervisor, I was tasked to review all of the documentation of the counselors under my leadership. I have seen the good, the bad and the ugly of notes.

I rejected notes daily from new counselors. I did not send them back to be mean or to give my counselors more work to do because our organization expected a lot of documentation in every client's chart. I sent notes back for three main reasons:

1) **A lot of typos (wrong names, wrong pronouns, misspellings).** To prevent this mistake, proofread your work.

2) **Not enough information given or lack of clarity.** Notes should be clear and concise. It is not about the word count; it is about the content. You have to support what you bill whether the session is 15 minutes or 60 minutes.

3) **Not following the DRIP or DAP structures of note taking. (See Appendix B)**

If you can avoid these three issues, you will have what it takes to write/present good notes! The templates I have included can be used in most clinical settings. Type of session notes are endless so these examples is not all encompassing yet they are the most used in the settings I have experienced.

Understanding your agency's documentation requirements, using proper formatting, managing your time and writing clear assessments/notes will: delay the onset of burn out, help build clinical confidence, and propel your career within healthcare systems.

The template sections are broken out to type of client/visit:

- **Scheduled Appointments:** Initial Appointment, Second Appointment, Individuals, Groups

- **Relapse/Recovery Plans:** Recovery Treatment Plan Update Appointment

- **Discharge Notes**

- **Miscellaneous Notes:** Case Management Notes (Outreach Call After a No Show)

SCHEDULED APPOINTMENTS

Note: *The strategy for the following scheduled appointments to reduce anxiety for both new client and the clinician by having a structured session and knowing what needs to be accomplished. It is important to not only gather information needed but to also assess how the client is responding to the assessment and to you.*

THE INITIAL APPOINMENT

DATA: Met with client for initial intake appointment where formal introductions were made, and client was able to express what led to current need for therapy. Client appeared calm and cooperative as well as open to engaging with Clinician.

INTERVENTION: Optional Intervention Choices Motivational Enhancement Therapy

Used reflective listening:

__Developed Discrepancies	__Rolled with Resistance	__Provided Helpful Advice or Direction
__Expressed Empathy	__Supported Choice and Self-Efficacy	__Developed a Clear Change Plan
__Reframed Problem	__Provided Motivation to Change	__Worked Collaboratively

RESPONSE: Currently **Low Risk** evidenced by no current suicidal or homicidal ideations, no auditory or visual hallucinations, no visible instability or risk for withdrawal. Mood and affect appropriate. Oriented 3x. Thoughts were logical and linear throughout interview. Maintained good eye contact.

Client appears to be in **Preparation Stage** (see Stages of Change Appendix A) of change evidenced by his/her (or other preferred pronoun) voluntary involvement in the mental health program and his/her agreement to meet with psychiatric prescriber for evaluation for potential medication management.

PLAN (Newly Assigned Patient): Main tasks in early sessions should focus on building rapport, encouraging Client to maintain mental health compliance by attending scheduled appointments and using positive coping strategies. Next session is schedule for (insert date) to begin treatment planning.

SECOND APPOINMENT

DATA: Met with client to continue gathering history as well as get description of current stressors and symptoms. Also, beginning the treatment planning process by allowing client to express her/his current stressors including (list the stressors).

Continued to gather understanding of Client's personal goals and priorities. She/he agreed to continue weekly appointments until she/he returns to her/his baseline level of functioning.

INTERVENTION: Building rapport, therapeutic alliance, and motivational interviewing.

RESPONSE: Client's disposition during today's session was _____. Currently Low Risk evidenced by no current suicidal or homicidal ideations, no auditor or visual hallucinations, no visible instability or risk for withdrawal. Mood and affect appropriate. Thoughts were logical and linear throughout interview ad maintained good eye contact.

PLAN: Next appointment to begin working on desired goals to stabilize symptoms and bring client to baseline level of functioning.

INDIVIDUAL SESSIONS

Note: The strategy for the following individual progress notes is to make sure that client work in and outside session is documented as well as their response(s) to clinical intervention(s) during the session. A therapist note should be thought of as a legal document and everything that is contained in the should be able to be answered by the author while under oath. For this and a myriad of other reasons, it is important to be circumspect regarding documentation.

INDIVIDUAL SESSION (for medication management clients only)

DATA: Client came to her/his scheduled appointment on time. She/He appears oriented 3x, stable, appropriate affect and disposition. She/He denies any distress. No apparent psychosis. She/He was able to clearly report her/his mood and behaviors since last appointment. She/He reports stability with medication compliance, and she/he acknowledged the need to continue with medication management. She/He identifies her/his (list person(s) as her/his main support and is looking forward to (list at least one future activity). Denies need for ongoing counseling services. Signed updated Medication Management Recover Plan (if available).

INTERVENTION: Treatment plan review, Acknowledgement of growth and stability

RESPONSE: Client's disposition during today's session was _____. Currently **Low Risk** evidenced by no current suicidal or homicidal ideations, no auditor or visual hallucinations, no visible instability or risk for withdrawal. Mood and affect appropriate. Thoughts were logical and linear throughout interview ad maintained good eye contact.

PLAN: Follow up as needed, continue medications as prescribed

INDIVIDUAL SESSION (for counseling clients)

DATA: Clinician met with Client for individual session. Clinician and client reviewed progress since last appointment. Client was able to articulate positive change efforts, current stressors as well as desire to remain emotionally stable. Client reports compliance with prescribed medication with symptom relief.

INTERVENTION: Building self-worth and esteem through empathetic listening and validation.

Optional intervention choices for trauma informed care:

__Built Trust	__Normalized Symptoms	__Focused on Resilience
__Developed Hope and Connection	__Identified and Managed Triggers	__Worked Collaboratively

RESPONSE: Client appears to have positive response to intervention and agreed to continue working on goals in session as well as at home. Currently, Low Risk evidenced by no current suicidal or homicidal ideations, no auditory or visual hallucinations, no visible instability or risk for withdrawal. Mood and affect appropriate. Oriented 3x. Thoughts were logical and linear throughout interview and maintained good eye contact. Client appears to be in **Maintenance Stage of Change** evidenced by her/his voluntary involvement in this mental health program, current medication compliance with stability, and his/her consistent appointments with psychiatric prescriber for medication management.

PLAN: Clinician will meet with client on _ (insert date) __.

INDIVIDUAL SESSION (client re-engages in treatment)

DATA: Clinician met with Client for individual session. Client was last seen on _____ and has cancelled or missed the past _____ individual sessions. Primary focus of session is to re-engage Client in treatment by discussing current stressors, barriers of treatment and level of motivation.

INTERVENTION: Rebuilding rapport and Therapeutic Alliance, Recovery Plan Update

RESPONSE: Client started session by indicating multiple reasons why he/she has missed several appointments. She/He appeared to seek approval and acceptance from Clinician despite noncompliance. Clinician used empathetic and reflective listening to decrease resistance and forge new working relationship. Client appears to have positive response to intervention and agreed to meet with Clinician for continued mental health treatment. Currently, Low Risk evidenced by no current suicidal or homicidal ideations, no auditory or visual hallucinations, no visible instability or risk for withdrawal. Mood and affect appropriate. Oriented 3x. Thoughts were logical and linear throughout interview and maintained good eye contact. Client appears to be in Preparation Stage of Change evidenced by new agreement to engage in mental health and substance abuse treatment and scheduling necessary appointments in advance. Client agreed to discuss medication concerns to prescriber at next appointment.

PLAN: Next appointment schedule on _____ to address strategies to limits and current barriers to treatment.

INDIVIDUAL SESSION WITH MAT CLIENT (Medication Assistance Treatment)

DATA: Clinician met with Client for individual session. Client was referred by his/her substance abuse counselor due to history of mental health diagnosis and current symptoms. Formal introductions were made and Clinician and Client reviewed history of substance abuse, clean time and relapses. Additionally, discussed how outstanding mental health concerns impact current drug treatment. Client was able to articulate positive change efforts and current stressors as well as a desire to remain emotionally stable and have consistent sobriety. Client has sent prescriber for medication management and currently report compliance with prescribed medication with symptom relief.

INTERVENTION: Building self-worth and esteem through empathic listening and validation; building rapport and Therapeutic Alliance.

RESPONSE: Client appears to have positive response to intervention and agreed to meet with Clinician for continued mental health treatment. Currently, Low Risk evidenced by no current suicidal or homicidal ideations, no auditory or visual hallucinations, no visible instability or risk for withdrawal. Mood and affect appropriate. Oriented 3x. Thoughts were logical and linear throughout interview and maintained good eye contact. Client appears to be in **Action Stage of Change** evidenced by readiness to work on treatment goals and making positive steps toward change through compliance with MAT requirements as well as seeking emotional stability through mental health treatment.

PLAN: Client will continue meeting for individual (and group if appropriate) sessions for MAT program. Client will have individual sessions one to two times per month with mental health clinician and continue medication management with prescriber.

COUPLE/FAMILY SESSION

DATA: Clinician met with client and spouse/family member for marital/family counseling session. Clinician and couple/family reviewed progress since last appointment. Both/All were able to articulate positive change efforts and current stressors as well as desire to remain committed to the relationship/family. Session used to reinforce positive communication.

INTERVENTION: Building effective communication and problem-solving skills.

Optional intervention choices for couple/family sessions:

__Asked Relational Questions	__Explored Couple/Family History and Relationships	__Raised Spouse's Interest in Each Other/ Raised Parents Interest in Child's Needs
__Reframed Problems Systematically	__Promoted Boundary Making	__Encouraged Support and Soothing
__Worked Collaboratively Using Couple/Family Competencies/Strengths	__Facilitated Parental Control/ Discipline	__Developed Strategies for Emotional Distress
__Directed/Changed Couple/Family Interactions	__Explored Emotional Experiences	__Facilitated Additional Support for Spouse/Parent

RESPONSE: Both/All appear open to suggestions by Clinician and report willingness to grow individually and relationally. No evidence of abuse during session.

PLAN: Next session/homework

GROUP SESSIONS

NOTE: *The strategy for the following group notes is that **Data** should consist of acknowledgement of each client's presence and appearance along with the objectives of the group. **Interventions** can be copied and pasted for all clients in the group. **Responses** should be different for each group member because each person will experience and interact with the group differently. **Plans** can be simply writing the topic or activity of the next group meeting and/or the date and can be the same for each client.*

<u>GROUP NOTES</u> – GENERAL

DATA: Client was present for today's Motivation Group. The topic was external versus internal motivations. Client was asked to describe motivation, write down what is their greatest motivation and what hinder them to be self-motivated. Client actively participated in the group by sharing his/her feelings and by giving feedback to fellow group members.

INTERVENTION: Defining motivation (internal/external)

RESPONSE: Client appears to have positive response to intervention evidenced by actively participating with little probing. Currently, Low Risk evidenced by no current suicidal or homicidal ideations, no auditory or visual hallucinations, no visible instability or risk for withdrawal. Mood and affect appropriate. Oriented 3x. Thoughts were logical and linear throughout group, allowed others to talk and maintained good eye contact. Client appears to be in **Action Stage of Change** evidenced by readiness to work on continued sobriety, emotional stability, personal goal setting and making positive steps towards change through compliance with MAT requirements.

PLAN: Client will continue meeting for group (and individual sessions if applicable) as scheduled. Next group will discuss __ (include topic) _ .

<u>GROUP NOTES</u> – Topic: SELF-ESTEEM

DATA: Client participated in today's group therapy. Today's topic was _____. Client was able to articulate the importance of building self-esteem as part of his/her recovery Client was (open and engaging), (resistant to share), (talkative), or (preoccupied). Client was engaged yet quiet; often found nodding his/her head in agreement.

INTERVENTION: Self-Esteem Worksheet, building self-worth and esteem through empathetic listening and validation, building rapport and Therapeutic Alliance, and facilitating group discussion/participation.

RESPONSE: Client appears to have positive response to intervention evidenced by active participation with little probing. Currently, Low Risk evidenced by no current suicidal or homicidal ideations, no auditory or visual hallucinations, no visible instability or risk for withdrawal. Mood and affect appropriate. Oriented 3x. Thoughts were logical and linear throughout group, allowed others to talk and maintained good eye contact. Client appears to be in Action Stage of Change evidenced by readiness to work on continued sobriety, emotional stability, personal goal setting and making positive steps towards change through compliance with treatment requirements.

PLAN: Continue weekly groups

<u>GROUP NOTES</u> – Topic: GRIEF

DATA: Client came to group on time and ready to participate. This was the first group and she/he was not shy to introduce her/himself to the facilitator or her/his peers. She/He shared her/his story and stated that she/he had come to today's group because

_____.

INTERVENTION: Building rapport, setting rules and group norms, explaining objectives for groups and giving room for each member to introduce themselves and share their stories. Normalizing feelings of grief. Psychoeducation – stages of grief and how compounded grief effect ability to cope.

RESPONSE: Client appears to have positive response to intervention evidenced by actively participating with little probing. Currently, Low Risk evidenced by no current suicidal or homicidal ideations, no auditory or visual hallucinations, no visible instability or risk for withdrawal. Mood and affect appropriate. Oriented 3x. Thoughts were logical and linear throughout group, allowed others to talk and maintained good eye contact

PLAN: Continue appointments as scheduled as scheduled. Client recommended to attend other groups.

RELAPSE/RECOVERY SESSIONS

Note: *The strategy of the following progress notes is to address recent or current relapse a client could be experiencing and how to remove barriers to their sobriety/stability. These notes can be useful for clinicians working in a detox treatment center or psychiatric hospital where you may often see your clients in Relapse Stage of Change.*

INITIAL RECOVERY PLAN

DATA: Clinician met with client for individual session to develop recovery plan. Client was able to express current concerns and treatment goals. Upon completion, plan was reviewed and signed. Client was given copy of Recovery Plan for record and review.

INTERVENTION: Recovery Plan, Supported Choice and Self efficacy, Normalized Symptoms, Focus on Resilience

RESPONSE: Client appears to have positive response to intervention and agreed to meet with Clinicians for continued mental health treatment. Client appears to be in Action Stage of Change evidenced by readiness to work on treatment goals and making positive steps towards change.

PLAN: Clinician will meet with Client to begin working on treatment plan goals and objectives.

RECOVERY TREATMENT PLAN (Follow up Appointment)

DATA: Clinician met with Client for individual session. Client was able to give update since previous session before reviewing treatment progress and update of current Recovery Plan. Client appeared calm and cooperative during interview. Acknowledgement of progress as well as identification of areas of continued concern were addressed. Necessary changes were made to the Recovery Plan and Client signed the document. Client was given a copy of Recovery Plan.

INTERVENTION: Recognition and validation. Recovery Plan update.

RESPONSE: Client appears to have a positive response to intervention and agreed to meet with Clinician for continued mental health treatment. Currently, Low Risk evidenced by no current suicidal or homicidal ideations, no auditory or visual hallucinations, no visible instability or risk for withdrawal. Mood and affect appropriate. Oriented 3x. Thoughts were logical and linear throughout interview and maintained good eye contact. Client appears to be in **Maintenance Stage of Change** evidenced by his/her ongoing voluntary involvement in this mental health program, current medication compliance with stability, and his/her consistent appointments with psychiatric prescriber for medication management.

PLAN: Clinician will meet with Client on _____. Client will discuss medication concerns with prescriber at next scheduled appointment (if meds are a part of treatment). (Optional: Homework _____)

*Addendum: If you work with people with co-occurring disorders or substance abuse disorders, you will deal with your share of resistant or ambivalent clients. It is also important to capture negative responses for your client to catalog their baseline, progress, and regression. Here is an example of a **RESPONSE** for a person offers resistance to treatment or a particular intervention:

Client appears defensive throughout the session. He/She appears frustrated with the recovery process and displays current hopelessness/helplessness in regard to successfully completing goals on the Recovery Plan. Interventions used to align with Client or re-engage seem to be null and void. Even though it does not appear that Client is upset with Clinician, they display dissatisfaction with process and display ambivalence in continuing. Currently, Low Risk evidenced by no current suicidal or homicidal ideations, no auditory or visual hallucinations, no visible instability or risk for withdrawal. Mood and affect appropriate. Oriented 3x. Thoughts were logical and linear throughout interview and maintained good *eye contact. Client appears to have returned to **Contemplative Stage of Change** evidenced by his/her uncertainty of the benefits of treatment and inability to admit current struggles to remain sober and emotionally stable.*

RECOVERY PLAN AFTER RELAPSE

DATA: Clinician met with Client for individual session. Client admits use of illicit substances during prior treatment plan period. Client understands lapse and relapse can be part of the recovery process and agrees to continue Outpatient Program until he/she is able to sustain from use of drugs and/or alcohol for at least twelve (12) weeks. Acknowledgement of progress as well as identification of areas of continued concern were addressed. Client verbalized new desire to remain sober despite current stressors and agreed to reach out to staff and/or natural supports (healthy family or friends) when prone to relapse. Necessary changes were made to Recovery Plan and Client signed document. Client was given a of Recovery Plan.

INTERVENTION: Recovery Plan Update, Motivational Interviewing, Highlighting Strengths, Review of Relapse Prevention Strategies, Wellness Plan/Safety Plan.

Optional Intervention Choices for Substance Abuse Treatment:

__Managing Triggers, Urges and Cravings	__Cognitive Restructuring/ Reframing	__Self-Efficacy Enhancement
__Managing High Risk Situations	__Developing Effective Coping Skills	__Developing a Balanced Lifestyle and Healthy Alternatives
__Addressing Social Pressure	__Social Skills Training	__Lapse Management

RESPONSE: Client appears to have positive response to intervention and agreed to meet with Clinician for continued substance abuse treatment. Currently, Low Risk evidenced by no current suicidal or homicidal ideations, no auditory or visual hallucinations, no visible instability or risk for withdrawal. Mood and affect appropriate. Oriented 3x. Thoughts were logical and linear throughout interview and maintained good eye contact. Client appears to be in **Preparation Stage of Change** evidenced by new agreement to engage in substance abuse treatment and scheduling necessary appointments in advance. Client agreed to discuss medication concerns with prescriber at next appointment.

PLAN: Clinician will meet with Client on _____. Clinician will continue to enhance and highlight client's strengths and positive efforts to encourage increased use of healthy coping strategies and relapse prevention activities. Client needs ongoing monitoring for medication efficacy and compliance. Clinician will promote regular attendance for individual counseling as well as prescriber appointments. Recommended client for group therapy or NA/AA to build additional peer supports and accountability.

DISCHARGE NOTES

NOTE: The strategy of the following discharge notes is to give a general blueprint of properly documenting a client's exit of treatment. This exit can be due to completion of specific program, a need for higher level of care, a need for lower level of care, against medical advice, a transfer to a new provider, or lack of participation in treatment.

DISCHARGE PLANNING SESSION – DISCHARGE TO NEW PROVIDER

DATA: Clinician met with Client for individual session to discuss treatment progress and discharge. Client was able to identify progress made in treatment as well as current stressors. Clinician and Client reviewed positive coping strategies, triggers and relapse prevention. Client articulated the importance of continued mental health care to support emotional stability. Client will be transferring to _____. Clinician had client sign consent to release information to new service provider. Clinician highlighted treatment successes to build on and assisted Client in identifying barriers to new treatment and how to overcome such barriers.

INTERVENTION: Discharge planning, closing session

RESPONSE: Client desires to receive local mental health services and was able to appropriate advocate for his/her needs. He/She understands what is expected from new service provider already (decided/called/has appointment) on/for continuity of care. Client is motivated to gain and maintain emotional stability and appears optimistic about transfer. Client appears to be in **Preparation Stage of Change** evidenced by new agreement to engage in same level of mental health treatment and scheduling necessary appointments in advance. Client agreed to discuss any medication or treatment concerns with new prescriber.

PLAN: Discharge/transfer. Care coordination, referrals as needed.

DISCHARGE PLANNING SESSION – MENTAL HEALTH (transferred to higher level of care)

DATA: Clinician met with Client for individual session to discuss treatment progress and discharge. Client was able to identify progress made in treatment as well as current stressors. Clinician and Client reviewed positive coping strategies, triggers and relapse prevention. Client articulated the importance of continued mental health care to support emotional stability. Client will be transferring to _____. Clinician had client sign consent to release information to new service provider.

Clinician highlighted treatment successes to build on and assisted Client in identifying barriers to new treatment and how to overcome such barriers.

INTERVENTION: Discharge planning, referrals as needed

RESPONSE: Client is in need of a higher level of care due to frequent episodes of needing inpatient hospitalization/crisis calls/detox. He/She understands what is expected from new service provider and already has appointment set up for continuity of care. Client is motivated to gain and maintain emotional stability and appears optimistic about transfer. Client appears to be in **Preparation Stage of Change** evidenced by new agreement to engage in higher level of mental health and substance abuse treatment and scheduling necessary appointments in advance. Client agreed to discuss medication concerns to prescriber at next appointment.

PLAN: Discharge/transfer. Care coordination as needed.

DISCHARGE PLANNING SESSION – SUBSTANCE ABUSE PROGRAM

DATA: Clinician met with Client for individual session to discuss treatment progress and discharge. Client was able to identify progress made in treatment as well as current stressors. Clinician and Client reviewed positive coping strategies, triggers and relapse prevention. Client expresses comfort in sobriety and denies desire to "use".

INTERVENTION: Discharge planning:

__Managing Triggers, Urges and Cravings	__Cognitive Restructuring/ Reframing	__Self-Efficacy Enhancement
__Managing High Risk Situations	__Developing Effective Coping Skills	__Developing a Balanced Lifestyle and Healthy Alternatives
__Addressing Social Pressure	__Social Skills Training	__Lapse Management

RESPONSE: Client appears to have positive response to intervention and agreed to continue to maintain sobriety by applying what was learned while attending substance abuse program. Currently, Low Risk evidenced by no current suicidal or homicidal ideations, no auditory or visual hallucinations, no visible instability or risk for withdrawal. Mood and affect appropriate. Oriented 3x. Thoughts were logical and linear throughout interview and maintained good eye contact. Client appears to be in Maintenance Stage of Change evidenced his/her voluntary involvement in this substance abuse program, current sobriety and the ability to develop new ways to cope without mood altering substances. Denies need for mental health services at this time.

PLAN: Discharged from program. Successful completion. Referral given – AA/NA meetings, other self-help groups, outpatient treatment.

MISCELLANEOUS NOTES

Note: The strategy for the following miscellaneous notes to illustrate the importance of documenting non-billable items that are pertinent to the client's treatment. There just so many things we do as therapists and clinicians that are not billable, so this, of course, is not an exhaustive list. These are the two non-billable notes I use most.

CASE MANAGEMENT NOTES (Outreach Call After a No Show)

Clinician called/texted number listed for **client name** (999-999-9999) after client missed scheduled appointment. Client chart noted ok to ID (leave message), so Clinician left name and company phone number without stating the type of appointment for confidentiality purposes.

NON-BILLABLE COLLATERAL CONTACTS

1. Clinician received call/email from client's (list relationship to client) stating:

2. Clinician called/emailed client's (list relationship to client) at client's request

3. Reference release form if needed before contact

4. Clinician called/texted/emailed client's emergency contact/ or parent (if minor) due to <u>(list reason for the interaction)</u>

5. Clinician completed requested documentation for <u>(list application, form, or any other type of paperwork requested by client)</u>

CONCLUSION

The elusive "Work/Life balance" is not impossible to achieve however it is difficult in societies that value productivity over wellbeing. Even as mental health providers, we often are given little time to heal from the issues we are dealing with. Many in helping professions often have similar struggles as their clients and have very little support, from employers, to maintain professional standards and expectations while embracing their personal journey of healing and recovery. Heal anyway.

It is important to note that there is only one you and your main priority must be your physical and mental wellbeing. Fight for your sanity, peace, and freedom. As you create personal strategies to gain balance and wellbeing and keep it, you are also giving others permission to do the same.

A key to work/life balance is to have a good time management and organization so you work effectively when you are scheduled to work and when you are off you are able to leave work at work knowing you did your best with the time allotted. You no longer operate out of guilt or at least limit those feelings.

You are no longer coming in early or leaving late to do unpaid work. You are no longer letting paperwork beat you down. You are no longer answering work emails on days off. You no longer will carry the burdens of a company or organization's lack of staff or resources to serve clients appropriately.

You are taking as much time as you need to recover from grief, loss, medical issues, and disappointments. You are going to use your personal and vacation days. You are going operate out of self-compassion and love.

Remember, you are not alone. Isolation is the enemy of growth and change. We are in this together. Only collective action will solve the current issues this world faces and we can start within our community of movers and shakers, helpers and healers.

I hope the tools, tips, templates in this book are useful in your practice and allows greater personal fulfillment doing clinical work.

This essential yet often-thankless work, needs you to be your best in all areas of your life. Hopefully, tackling your paperwork with this approach will inspire other positive changes in your clinical practice.

Check out the other books in this series and good luck in your future endeavors!

All Currently Available on Kindle and Amazon

- The Goal Chaser's Guide to Clinical Practice by Lakeeya Homsey, LICSW

- Treatment Planning Made Simple by Lakeeya Homsey, LICSW

- I Quit! A Book about Burnout by Walter Homsey, LCSW and Lakeeya Homsey, LICSW

APPENDIX A

Prochaska & DiClemente's Stages of Change

Pre-Contemplation- No intention of changing behavior

Contemplation- Aware that a problem exists but has no commitment to action

Preparation- Intent on taking action to address or fix the problem

Action- Active Modification of Behaviors

Maintenance- Sustained change. New healthier behaviors replace old unhealthy behaviors

Relapse- Fall back to old patterns of behavior

For More Information about the Stages of Change and how it is utilized in clinical treatment, these are helpful links:

https://online.yu.edu/wurzweiler/blog/prochaska -and-diclementes-stages-of-change-model-for-social-workers-2

https://sphweb.bumc.bu.edu/otlt/mph-modules/sb/behavioralchangetheories/behavioral changetheories6.html

APPENDIX B

Good Notes Have Good Structure

DIRP (Data, Intervention, Response, Plan)

or DAP (Data, Assessment, Plan) Notes

We will focus on the **DIRP** note taking process. The only difference is that some practices combine the **IR** into **A** for Assessment.

*D*ATA (Observations)

- ✓ **Who, what when, where, why**? Example, Clinician met with the Client in the office for an individual session. Client arrives on time and appropriately dressed for the weather. Clinician and Client reviewed progress since last appointment. Client was able to articulate positive change efforts, current stressors as well as the desire to remain emotionally stable. Client reports compliance with prescribed medication with symptom relief.

INTERVENTION (Techniques, Strategies, Paperwork)

✓ Whatever attempted or completed in a session goes here. **TIP:** If active recovery plan is available, cut and paste the interventions from the plan.

✓ Use interpersonal therapy techniques to explore and resolve issues surrounding grief, role disputes, role transitions and social skills deficits. Provide support and strategies for resolving identified interpersonal issues.

RESPONSE (Clinical Impression)

✓ What is the Client's reaction to your intervention? What is your overall clinical impression?

✓ Stage of change, risk level, current stability

PLAN (Follow-Up)

✓ Next appointment, next objective to work on, paperwork needed, homework given and any case management.

Made in the USA
Monee, IL
15 June 2024

59969322R00031